Celebrity Biographies

Kanye West

HIP-HOP STAR

GRETCHEN WEICKER

Enslow Publishers, Inc.
40 Industrial Road
Box 398
Berkeley Heights, NJ 07922
USA
http://www.enslow.com

Library of Congress Cataloging-in-Publication Data
Weicker, Gretchen.
 Kanye West : hip-hop star / Gretchen Weicker.
    p. cm. — (Hot celebrity biographies)
 Includes bibliographical references and index.
 Summary: "Read about best-selling hip-hop artist Kanye West. From his childhood dreams to becoming a star, find out what he has planned for the future"—Provided by publisher.
  ISBN-13: 978-0-7660-3214-9
  ISBN-10: 0-7660-3214-0
 1. West, Kanye—Juvenile literature. 2. Rap musicians—United States—Biography—Juvenile literature. I. Title.
 ML3930.W42W44 2009
 782.421649092—dc22
 [B]
                            2008026466

Paperback ISBN-13: 978-0-7660-3629-1
Paperback ISBN-10: 0-7660-3629-4

Printed in the United States of America

10 9 8 7 6 5 4 3 2 1

To our readers: We have done our best to make sure all Internet Addresses in this book were active and appropriate when we went to press. However, the author and the publisher have no control over and assume no liability for the material available on those Internet sites or on other Web sites they may link to. Any comments or suggestions can be sent by e-mail to comments@enslow.com or to the address on the back cover.

♲ Enslow Publishers, Inc., is committed to printing our books on recycled paper. The paper in every book contains 10% to 30% post-consumer waste (PCW). The cover board on the outside of each book contains 100% PCW. Our goal is to do our part to help young people and the environment too!

Photographs: Michael Kim/AP Images, 1; Matt Sayles/AP Images, 4, 11, 26; Nathan Denette/AP Images, 7, 31; Tina Fineberg/AP Images, 8; Jeff Christensen/AP Images, 9, 36; Brian Kersey/AP Images, 13; Mark Gail/ The Washington Post, 15; Jim Cooper/AP Images, 17, 25; MJ Kim/Getty Images, 18; Damian Dovarganes/AP Images, 20; Reed Saxon/AP Images, 21; Kevork Djansezian/AP Images, 23; John Smock/AP Images, 29; Joe Cavaretta/AP Images, 33; Matt Dunham/AP Images, 34; Chris Pizzello/AP Images, 40; Ian West/AP Images, 43

Cover photo: Kanye West performs on the *Good Morning America* concert series in 2005.
Michael Kim/AP Images.

Contents

The One and Only Kanye

When Kanye West was born on June 8, 1977, his parents knew he would be their only child. Kanye was born in Atlanta, Georgia, to Ray West and Donda Williams West. He was special to them, so they wanted him to have a special name. For his first name, they used a word from the Swahili language that means "the only one." They chose Omari for his middle name, which means "wise one."

Kanye Omari West did in fact seem wise. His mother, Donda, wrote about what the hip-hop star was like as a child in her book *Raising Kanye*. Donda wrote that Kanye's baby eyes "spoke" and showed he had an "old soul." But he was active too. She remembered him trying to climb out of his crib. Once he even flopped out of his crib onto the floor.

For most of the first year of Kanye's life, the little family of three lived together in Atlanta. His father, Ray, was a professional photographer. His son was so special to him that he took photos of every big first. He also photographed every visitor who came to see baby Kanye.

◀ *Kanye West has spent most of his life living up to the meaning of his name.*

ALL ABOUT KANYE

Born: June 8, 1977
Birth name: Kanye Omari West
Parents: Ray and Donda West
Height: 5 feet, 8 inches
Nicknames: Ye; The Konman
Mascot: Teddy bear
Favorite band: Franz Ferdinand
Interests: Dancing, art, basketball, fashion, movies, video games
First job: Telemarketer
Pet: Fish

When Kanye was three years old, his parents decided to get a divorce. His father found less and less time for his family as he tried to start his own photography studio. First his parents separated. Then in 1980, Kanye and his mom moved to Chicago without Ray.

From that time on, Kanye tried to look out for his mom. If she was sad, Kanye tried to make her feel better. As an adult, he even wrote a song for her called "Hey Mama." He sings that as a child he wanted to love her until she didn't hurt any more.

While Kanye was growing up, his dad also cared for him. Kanye lived with his mom in Chicago during the school year. He lived with his father in Atlanta every summer, Christmas, and spring break. This allowed Kanye's father to stay connected to him.

▲ *Kanye West performs at MTV studios in 2006.*

BRIGHT AND BOSSY

In Chicago, Kanye started going to preschool. His mother admitted that he sometimes got into trouble at school. She thought one reason for this could be that he was an only child. At school, he was scolded for always wanting his own way.

His kindergarten teacher complained that he did not work well with others. His aunt and uncle also noticed this bossy behavior. They remember a time at the park when Kanye was six years old. Kanye insisted that the ducks do what he said.

He yelled at the ducks because they were not quacking the right way.

When he wasn't getting into trouble, Kanye was a talented student. He loved to draw cartoons with his big box of sixty-four crayons. He also did well with writing and reading. Kanye's father once told a reporter that this was because both parents encouraged him. Ray and Donda always talked to Kanye as if he were an adult.

▲ Kanye West has been doing things his own way since he was a child.

As he got older, Kanye could only watch television once he finished his homework. Both of his parents were college teachers and cared very much about schoolwork. His mother taught English, and his father taught photography. On days that his mother couldn't be home right after school, Kanye would go straight to her office. He often did his homework there.

A WORLD OF EXPERIENCE

When he was just ten years old, Kanye had the opportunity to study in another country. In 1987, Kanye's mother took a one-year teaching job in the city of Nanjing, China. Kanye was able to go with her. Kanye attended an international school there. At school, he made friends from all over the world. Just like millions of Chinese people, Kanye and his mom went everywhere on bikes. He learned to speak Chinese from neighborhood children. Kanye and his mother also traveled to Hong Kong and Thailand.

Together, they learned a lot about life in a different part of the world. The weather in China was even colder than in Chicago, but the classrooms in China were unheated. Students wore their coats and gloves inside. His classmates' gloves seemed odd to Kanye because the fingers were cut out. All Kanye had were typical American winter gloves. But his Chinese teacher wouldn't let him wear those. When the teacher tried to pull the gloves off Kanye's hands,

▶ *Kanye West is known for his sometimes preppy style of dressing.*

9

Kanye kicked the teacher. Kanye's mother had to meet with his teacher to talk about his behavior. A Chinese interpreter helped the mother and the teacher understand each other. After the meeting, Kanye had to apologize to his teacher.

Kanye's mom thought these childhood experiences helped shape the person he turned out to be. His love for words came from her, and his interest in art and design came from his father. His family also helped shape his religious beliefs.

As he got older, Kanye became even more interested in drawing cartoons, designing clothes, and dancing. Most of all, though, he loved music. At age fourteen, the future hip-hop artist got his first electronic keyboard. He began to create his own rap lyrics and beats. His talent impressed his mother. "I never imagined that I would be the mother of someone quite as unique as Kanye West," she wrote in *Raising Kanye*. She believed he was meant to do something very special in the world.

Father Figures

Ray West, Kanye's father, also believes that his son has powerful gifts. Ray thinks Kanye has been given these gifts so that he can help others. He sees pieces of himself in his son. Ray West has always tried to give back to the world. He has talked to Kanye about doing the same.

KANYE ON KANYE

On his music: "My music isn't just music—it's medicine. I want my songs to touch people, to give them what they need."

On his busy, active lifestyle: "If I was more complacent [laid-back] and I let things slide, my life would be easier, but you all wouldn't be as entertained."

On his talent: "I'm nowhere as good as Jay-Z, Eminem, or Nas. So I compensate [make up for it] with star power, sheer energy, entertainment, videos, really good outfits, and overwhelmingly, ridiculously dope tracks."

Ray West encourages his son to use his money for good causes. "I wanted him to associate with something positive," Ray said in an interview in 2006 with the *Washington Post* newspaper.

Kanye's dad also grew up in a religious family that taught him to care about other people. Ray came from a military family that lived in many places. He saw people in different living conditions. When Ray went to college in the 1960s, he fought for civil rights for black people. As a teacher during the 1970s, he taught photography and sociology at several colleges. He also was an award-winning newspaper photographer for the *Atlanta Journal-Constitution*. Now Ray cares for others as a Christian family counselor.

FATHER-SON PROJECTS

In November 2006, the father and son began a major project on behalf of people all over the world. Their project centered on the United Nations World Water Day. Women and children in some areas of the world must walk as much as six miles per day to get clean water, according to the United Nations. Kanye West and his dad wanted to let people know about this problem. They opened a café in Lincoln Park, Maryland, near Ray West's counseling office. The café offers food, Internet access, and live music. To draw attention to the goals of the United Nations, the café sells purified water with its meals or in containers to take home. It also sells purification equipment to use in homes or offices.

In 2007, Kanye and his dad walked together at a World Water Day rally. The two walked with other interested citizens and county officers. They walked six miles around a track at a city park in Lincoln Park, Maryland. The day also was the official grand opening celebration of Ray West's Good Water Store and Internet Café. Marchers and customers could have

▶ *Kanye West gives an interview in 2007.*

WORLD WATER DAY

sandwiches and smoothies. They also drank purified water to remind everyone of World Water Day's purpose. On that day, Kanye told the local news that he and his dad "had been talking about this for years."

LIKE FATHER, LIKE SON

Kanye's mother once told a Chicago radio station that both men are alike because they're smart, creative, and against injustice. Kanye uses his own set of skills to follow in his father's footsteps. He takes a stand by writing lyrics, composing music, and producing videos about issues that are important to him.

For example, Ray once asked his son about the lyrics of Kanye's song, "Diamonds from Sierra Leone." Kanye has said that he thought he was just doing a rap about jewelry, until his dad and friends told him about "blood diamonds." Then he learned about the African children used in some diamond mines and the bloody fighting over the jewels. Knowing this, the lyrics became more important to him.

Kanye decided to use his music video for the song to let others know. At the end of the video, African children run into a church for safety. Kanye is playing the organ at the altar and saying, "Diamonds are forever, and forever is a mighty long time." The video was supposed to draw attention to the African children affected by the diamond trade. Kanye told a magazine interviewer that songs like this one help get the attention of kids. "I throw up historical subjects in a way that makes kids want to learn about them," he said.

▼ *Ray West, Kanye's father, displays a bottle of purified water from the Good Water Store and Internet Café.*

OTHER ROLE MODELS

Ray wasn't the only role model for his son. Kanye also speaks proudly of both of his grandfathers. Both men had independent personalities and strong religious faith. They taught him self-confidence (and how to iron his own shirts!). He also is grateful for his uncles, who helped raise him. And he looked up to a teacher and family friend who helped build his self-discipline.

Kanye remembers high school friends who looked for role models in the "thug life." But he did not need to do that. Sometimes Kanye has been called a "mama's boy" because of his close relationship to his mother. But he never forgets to name the important men who gave his life a sense of purpose.

▶ *Both Kanye West's parents shaped the person that he became.*

Mother's Love

Kanye wrote the song "Hey Mama" to honor his mother, Donda. In a television interview, he described both parents as his "everything." But Donda was his biggest influence because he spent more time with her. He wrote "Hey Mama" in 2005 when he was twenty-seven. The lyrics speak touching words of apology, pride, and love.

His lyrics explain why he wanted to apologize. He mentions that he acted like a fool, but most of all he's sorry he dropped out of college against her wishes. Donda was disappointed because she had spent her career as a college professor. In "Hey Mama," he promises to return to college. The song goes on to thank her for believing in Kanye's music.

In "Hey Mama," Kanye also thanks his mother for all the little things she did to comfort him. He mentions the homemade chicken soup she would make him when he was sick, and the training wheels she got him for his bike. In her book *Raising Kanye*, Donda describes an incident involving that bike. The Wests lived in a dangerous Chicago neighborhood

◀ *Kanye West and his mother, Donda West, attend a book signing for* Raising Kanye *in London in 2007.*

▲ *Kanye West and his mother sing during* The Ellen DeGeneres Show *in 2006.*

when Kanye was a child. One day, some older boys tried to steal his bike. As Kanye tried to ride away, they slashed his tires. Soon after that, he and his mother moved into a safer area.

MAMA'S BOY

After Kanye received his first keyboard, his mother allowed him to set up a music studio in his bedroom. For the next six years, he wrote and produced music for school talent shows and for young local Chicago rappers. In middle school and high school, he had his own rap groups. They were called The Go-Getters and later State of Mind. Sometimes Kanye even designed costumes and planned dance moves for the rap groups.

Because her influence on his life has always been so strong, Kanye was sometimes teased in high school. Even a newspaper headline once called him a "mama's boy." But Kanye never minded. In the introduction he wrote for his mother's book, he writes, "Because of who she is, I am able to be who I am."

In *Raising Kanye*, Donda West lists the qualities she tried to have as a mother. They included "love, faith, patience . . . high expectations, good communication, and trust." In return, Kanye hoped to be a good son. "Hey Mama," he sings to her, "I just want you to be proud of me."

In 1997, his mother asked him to move out. Kanye was twenty years old. Donda always had faith in him and his music. But by that time, the musicians and music equipment were taking over the house. Moving out of his mother's house became a turning point for Kanye. He began to focus totally on his music. In 2004, he released his first successful album, *The College Dropout*. This success made his mother proud.

Kanye is proud of his mother's own success, too. For his Grammy performance of

▶ *Kanye West and his mother hold his three Grammys in 2006.*

21

"Hey Mama," he added the lines that she was "unbreakable, unmistakable . . . highly capable." He especially admired her hard work as a teacher.

HIS MOTHER'S SUPPORT

Kanye attended the American Academy of Art for one semester with an art scholarship. Then he decided he did not want to be an artist and transferred to Chicago State University. There, he majored in English, the department his mother chaired.

In his third semester of college, Kanye decided it wasn't for him. He wanted to focus on his music career instead. Donda was disappointed at first, but she came to believe her son would still accomplish something big in the world. She realized that Kanye knew what he wanted to do with his life and encouraged him to go for it.

Of course, Kanye didn't become a hip-hop superstar overnight. His first job was as a telemarketer, someone who sells products to people over the phone. Kanye had always been good at talking, and he did very well at it. He even called his mom once to give her his sales pitch. Kanye was so good at it, Donda didn't even know it was her son until he said so. Still, his career as a salesman was short. Bigger things were in store.

SAYING GOOD-BYE

Donda West died suddenly on November 10, 2007. Her heart failed the day after complicated surgery. Now the song "Hey Mama" is even more emotional for Kanye. On February 10, 2008, he sang "Hey Mama" softly in front of thousands of people at the fiftieth annual Grammy Awards.

Kanye was wearing all black and kneeling on the stage under a single spotlight. He performed with the word "mama" shaved into his hair. Later that same night he dedicated his award for Best Rap Album to her. He asked the studio orchestra to stop playing while he spoke about his mama.

▼ *Kanye West honored his mother with a performance at the 2008 Grammy Awards.*

A memorial service for Donda West took place in November 2007 at Chicago State University, where she taught for twenty-four years. There, her coworkers described her as a teacher who treated all people with dignity. This career in education gave Kanye and his mom a safe and happy life.

Just after Kanye's mother died, he told a reporter that he was surprised when his own songs ended up helping him. His 2008 Grammy-winning song is titled "Stronger." In its lyrics, he used words similar to a famous quotation from a German philosopher: "What doesn't kill me makes me stronger." West has faced many challenges, including his mother's death. But he believes these challenges have made him stronger.

HIP-HOP CULTURE

Kanye West has left his own mark on the hip-hop world with the way he dresses and his style of music. But he is still very much a part of a culture that has been around for more than thirty years. Hip-hop started in the 1970s in the Bronx, a section of New York City. Young people in urban areas started rapping on street corners, in dance clubs, and at parties. Often they made up the lyrics as they went—from nonsense rhymes to shout-outs to their friends. DJs took records and scratched them back and forth to create rhythms.

Soon, hip-hop became more than a kind of music. It was a lifestyle. Dancers started wearing baggy and colorful clothes to create a hip-hop look. Break dancing also became popular for its hip-hop moves. Large artwork called graffiti appeared on city buildings and transportation. Hip-hop grew into more than a style of music. It became more popular with television shows such as *The Fresh Prince of Bel-Air,* starring Will Smith, and rappers like MC Hammer and Vanilla Ice. While some people don't like the lyrics and videos, hip-hop culture has been an important influence for the past thirty years.

▲ *Kanye poses on a rooftop in New York with the Empire State Building in the background.*

Triumphs

Kanye often credits his family and his faith for all the good things in his life. Other successful rappers from the world of hip-hop sometimes sing about poverty, violence, and drug abuse. Kanye has said he never lived that kind of "thug life." But he has had his own struggles even before the death of his mother. His words make it clear that he learned from these challenges and turned them into triumphs.

One of his first tests was making it on his own after his mother asked him to move out at age twenty. Donda wrote that she wasn't rejecting her son or his dreams. It was the constant flow of people and the loud music that drove her to it.

Kanye also was kicked out by his first landlord in Chicago. The landlord complained about the noise from the musicians practicing and recording. Kanye finally found a place to live in Newark, New Jersey.

◄ *Kanye West overcame several setbacks to become the hip-hop superstar he is today.*

THE HISTORY OF RAP MUSIC

If you're a fan of Kanye West and other hip-hop stars, you might think of rap as being a very new kind of music. Just think of the technology used to produce today's rap music! But actually, the idea of speaking with rhyme and rhythm goes back to ancient times.

Early peoples all around the world chanted, prayed, sang, and told stories long before there was any way to write them down. Rhyme and rhythm made it easier to memorize long pieces. Traditionally, poems and songs have both rhythm and rhyme. Historians who study language also can trace the word "rap," meaning "to speak," back for hundreds of years.

Emcees in the hip-hop clubs of the 1970s began to speak in rhyme over their amplified beats. By the 1980s, rap artists were receiving recording contracts. This music style became popular around the world. Rap lyrics can be about everything from urban life to world problems.

SEVERAL SETBACKS

By 2000, Kanye was making a living producing the work of other hip-hop artists. But no one hired him to record his own songs. Twice, he met with men in charge of famous record companies. But they did not sign him to their labels. One of the most disappointing rejections happened in California.

Kanye was so excited to be flown there by Sony Records. Sony had a limousine pick him up at the airport. West sat in the executives' offices and tried to answer their questions. But when the interview was over, they said thanks, shook his hand, and said good-bye.

They made no plans for even getting Kanye back to the airport. He was on his own again.

Around the same time, Kanye was supposed to perform during a big hip-hop concert in Chicago called "Roc the Mic." But at the moment he was supposed to step on stage, the music switched to another singer's performance without warning. Kanye was left standing in the dark.

KANYE'S WAY

Kanye believes his early rejections came about because of his image. He was not a typical hip-hop artist. Despite this, he finally put out his own album in 2004. His friend, rapper Jay-Z, helped him get it released.

Finally, Kanye received some recognition. His album *The College Dropout* was nominated for Album of the Year at the Grammy Awards, but didn't win. Still, Kanye did win

▶ *Kanye West performs at a party in 2007.*

KANYE'S CREDITS

Kanye West has had three hit albums so far, including *The College Dropout* (2004), *Late Registration* (2005), and *Graduation* (2007). He has produced songs and albums for many other performers, including Jay-Z's *The Blueprint* (2001). Other artists he has produced music for include Alicia Keys, Janet Jackson, Mobb Deep, Scarface, and Jermaine Dupri.

Kanye's own songs have appeared on the soundtracks of a number of television shows, such as *Medium* and *Entourage*. He also performs on the soundtracks of several hit movies, including *Mission: Impossible III, Inside Man,* and *Fantastic Four*. He recently played himself in the 2008 movie *The Love Guru.*

Grammy awards for Best Rap Song, for "Jesus Walks," and for Best Rap Album. *The College Dropout* also was chosen as one of the top fifty albums of 2004 by *Rolling Stone* magazine.

Kanye released the album *Late Registration* in 2005. Knowing how hard he had worked, he felt he had a good chance of winning the 2006 Grammy Award for Album of the Year. Again, he didn't win. Next, he believed that his video for "Touch the Sky" could win the 2006 European MTV Best Video award. He did not win that either. At the 2007 MTV Awards, he lost all five categories for which he was nominated. With each loss he complained angrily and publicly. "You can never take away from the amount of work I put into it," he said.

Still, Kanye prides himself on working hard and staying confident. So he did not give up. In 2008, he was nominated for eight Grammy awards. That was more than any other artist. Kanye won in four categories. He took Best Rap Album for *Graduation*. The song "Stronger" was named Best Solo, and "Good Life" was chosen as Best Rap Song. He also won Best Rap Performance by a Duo or Group for "Southside." Kanye performed the song with the rapper Common.

▼ *Kanye West performs at MTV Studios in Canada in 2006.*

SURVIVAL AND SUCCESS

Kanye almost didn't have the chance to accomplish any of this. In 2002, he almost died in a terrible car wreck. His mother described it in her book. On the night of October 23, 2002, Kanye fell asleep at the wheel. He had been driving back to his hotel from a recording studio in Los Angeles. His car crashed head-on into another car. The other driver's legs were broken. Kanye had to be cut from his car. Kanye spoke to his mother on the phone at the accident scene. He let her know he was all right.

When Kanye got to the hospital, doctors found that his face was broken in three places. His head was so swollen, he was unrecognizable to family and friends. It took almost four hours of surgery to put him back together. For the following six weeks, his mouth was wired shut. All he could do was eat and talk through the wire.

Kanye believes his survival was a gift. His song "Through the Wire" talks about how he overcame disaster. Toward the end of the song, he sings, "But I'm a champion, so I turned tragedy to triumph." In interviews, he has said that God protected him so he could go on making music. Sometimes, he feels God in the studio with him, he says.

Kanye has risen above many obstacles. He returned to health after a horrible car wreck. Now, he also carries the sorrow of losing his mother. Kanye has said that his music is about more than winning awards. He writes songs to help people with their problems.

▼ Kanye West was named Rap Artist of the Year at the 2004 Billboard Awards.

Anything but Typical

The story of Kanye's life is told within his songs. But he says that his life goal is "to put out positive energy" because he believes his life was spared so that he could help others. Kanye sometimes calls his work a mission that only he can accomplish.

Kanye stands out in the world of hip-hop because he breaks its stereotypes. Many people have written that he is "not a typical rapper." Since the 1970s, rap songs and videos have usually shown aggressive young black men. They wear big clothes with bold jewelry and drive fancy cars. The scenery shows run-down city neighborhoods where people struggle with poverty and drugs.

Many parents and teachers object to rap lyrics because they are often full of curse words, rude references to women, and violence.

◀ *Kanye West performs in London in 2007.*

Some fans are glad for an honest, even angry, picture of social problems. But critics say rap can glorify the "thug life."

KANYE'S STYLE

Kanye expanded rap music to include what one journalist called the "nerd life." For example, he doesn't look the part of a "thug." He dresses conservatively, likes wearing backpacks, and uses a teddy bear as his trademark. These are not a part of rap music's tough image.

Kanye makes jokes about his own appearance. In a 2005 MTV television interview, he laughed that his smile would "break [his] cool." He joked that his fitted shirt could look like a "suction cup T-shirt." On that same show, he described his look as that of a professional producer with Italian shoes. He complained that on another television broadcast, his "pink and brown outfit" wasn't shown.

Kanye is creating his own fashion line to reflect his unusual style. It features such colors as pink, lavender, and light blue. These rainbow colors are not traditionally part of the rap video world. His mother described the look in her book: "I guess that backpack, along with everything else—the preppy clothes, not being a former drug dealer or [gang member], or rapping about guns and killing—made it all stick."

Kanye has said that his appearance and middle-class life made some people think he would not make it as a rapper. In one rap song, he calls these people "dreamkillers" because they rejected him and his music. Of course, he has become successful by defying stereotypes. That's why he wrote "Everything I Am," the popular rap that goes: "Everything I'm not made me everything I am."

NEW SOUND

His music does not fit the typical sound of hip-hop either. Even Kanye's view about the role of hip-hop is not typical. He believes his unusual musical sound and honest words can change American culture. "That's what hip-hop is all about," he says. "Good music can break through anything."

Kanye wants to reach out to listeners' emotions with his music. He hopes that his lyrics will show them that someone hears their pain. He uses instruments uncommon in rap music, such as violins, harps, or harpsichords. Sometimes, he invites singers to join him, or he includes samples from vocalists who are not a part of the rap world. For example, the tenor Adam Levine's voice floats high over the top of Kanye's rap lyrics in the song "Heard 'Em Say." The same song also has an unusual video. It is a hand-drawn, black-and-white cartoon.

MAKING WAVES

Kanye's lyrics and public remarks often attack injustice. He is outspoken about political issues and his religious faith. Kanye often writes lyrics and designs videos that question American values. More than one video shows Americans being more worried about possessions than about each other.

Sometimes, his controversial words can make people angry. For instance, on national television in 2005 he criticized President George W. Bush. He said that Bush did not take care of the black citizens of New Orleans who were stranded after Hurricane Katrina. Some people applauded his opinion, but others were upset.

Kanye's faith also did not seem to fit with what record companies expected from rap music. According to lines from his song "Jesus Walks," music executives told him, "You can rap about anything except for Jesus." Kanye replies in the song, "That means . . . if I talk about God, my record won't get played, huh?" Of course, this didn't turn out to be true. His Grammy-winning records are played plenty. And in two of his videos, Kanye portrays himself as a minister. He raps from the pulpit in the "Jesus Walks" video. And in the "Diamonds from Sierra Leone" video, he is the minister of music playing the organ while children run toward him in a church. Hovering angels appear in some of his videos, too. In "Heard 'Em Say," one angel looks like Kanye.

STAYING POSITIVE

Kanye wants his positive energy to reach as many people as possible. That's why his efforts go beyond his music. He is involved in so many different things that some people think he is overconfident or arrogant. For example, he is working to develop a clothing and accessories line. He also talked to television producers about starring in a series.

He has set up a charitable foundation. It supports such efforts as a school dropout prevention program called Loop Dreams. This program will donate video production software to public school students. He has written a regular fashion column for *Complex* magazine, and he wrote a book called *Thank You and You're Welcome*. The book contains Kanye's ideas and stories about how to be successful.

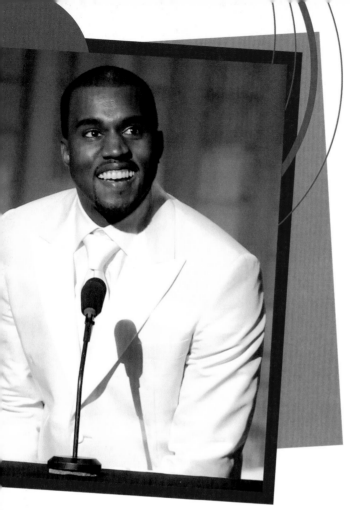

▲ *Kanye West accepts an NAACP Image Award in 2005.*

Why has Kanye taken on so much? "We gotta push the envelope," Kanye explained in a 2005 interview with MTV. He believes people are being brought together through the influence of hip-hop culture and rap music.

Kanye isn't the only one who believes in the power of hip-hop. In 2008, the Smithsonian Institute in Washington, D.C., featured an exhibit about the impact of hip-hop. During the same year, the Museum of Contemporary Art in Detroit, Michigan, had the "Holy Hip-Hop" exhibit. Both shows displayed large portraits of well-known rap artists. Kanye's picture showed him leaning forward and wearing a backpack. The museum directors said they wanted to get people talking about the ways hip-hop music influences how people think of wealth and power.

AWARDS

Kanye West's work has been recognized by many award shows and organizations. Here is a sampling of his honors:

2008
- Won four Grammy Awards: Best Rap Solo Performance, Best Rap Performance by a Duo or Group, Best Rap Song, Best Rap Album

2007
- Won two BET Hip-Hop Awards: Best Live Performance, Best Hip-Hop Video

2006
- Won three Grammy Awards: Best Rap Song, Best Rap Album, and Best Rap Solo Performance

- Won Two Billboard R&B/Hip-Hop Awards: Top Rap Album, Hot Rap Track of the Year

2005
- Won three Grammy Awards: Best Rap Song, Best Rap Album, and Best R&B Song
- Won MTV Video Music Award for Best Male Video

Not everyone agrees with Kanye West's opinions. But he still plans to use the power of hip-hop music to make a difference in the world. He's not afraid to say what he thinks about issues or about his own talents. One writer described Kanye as totally "unafraid" after the car accident in which the performer nearly died. Kanye also has talked about the powerful lesson he learned from that experience. "If you have the opportunity to play this game called life," he said in his 2006 Grammy speech, "you have to appreciate every moment."

Kanye West continues to make waves in the hip-hop world ▶
with his unusual look, music, and personality.

Timeline

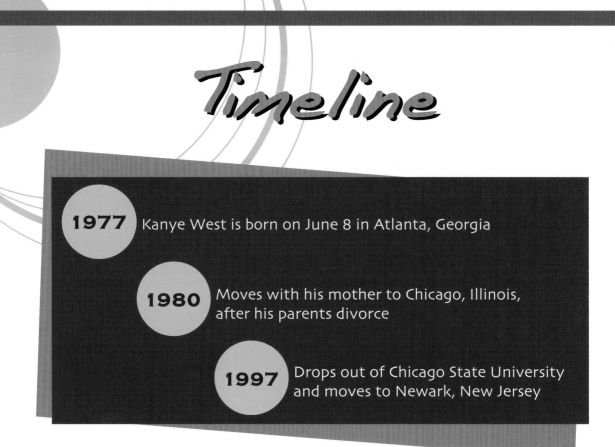

1977   Kanye West is born on June 8 in Atlanta, Georgia

1980   Moves with his mother to Chicago, Illinois, after his parents divorce

1997   Drops out of Chicago State University and moves to Newark, New Jersey

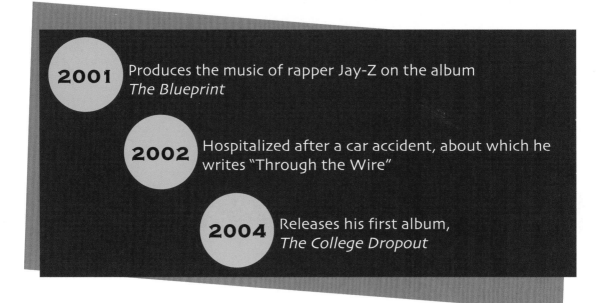

2001   Produces the music of rapper Jay-Z on the album *The Blueprint*

2002   Hospitalized after a car accident, about which he writes "Through the Wire"

2004   Releases his first album, *The College Dropout*

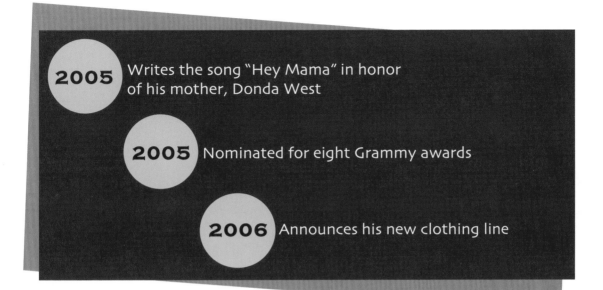

2005 Writes the song "Hey Mama" in honor of his mother, Donda West

2005 Nominated for eight Grammy awards

2006 Announces his new clothing line

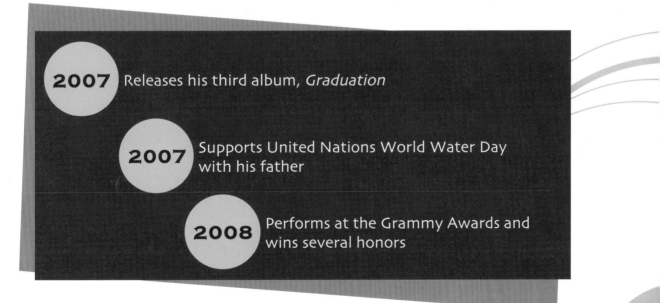

2007 Releases his third album, *Graduation*

2007 Supports United Nations World Water Day with his father

2008 Performs at the Grammy Awards and wins several honors

Further Info

BOOKS

Baker, Soren. *The History of Rap and Hip-Hop*. Chicago: Lucent Books, 2006.

Simons, Rae. *Kanye West*. Broomall, PA: Mason Crest, 2007.

Wells, Peggy Sue. *Kanye West*. Hockessin, DE: Mitchell Lane Publishers, 2008.

INTERNET ADDRESSES

Dr. Donda West Foundation
http://www.kanyewestfoundation.org

World Water Day
http://www.worldwaterday.org

Glossary

aggressive—Showing fierce or threatening behavior.

harpsichord—A keyboard instrument that looks like a small piano.

hip-hop—A style of dancing, art, music, and dress that originated in urban areas and became popular through break dancing, graffiti, and rap music.

purification—The process of making something pure or clean.

rap—A type of song in which the words are spoken in a rhythmical way to a musical background.

sociology—The study of the way people live together in different societies.

stereotype—An overly simple picture of a person, group, or thing.

tenor—The highest natural adult male voice.

United Nations—A worldwide organization that promotes international peace and cooperation.

Index